Thomas Annan

# The painted windows of Glasgow Cathedral

A series of forty-three photographs

Thomas Annan

**The painted windows of Glasgow Cathedral**
*A series of forty-three photographs*

ISBN/EAN: 9783742843425

Manufactured in Europe, USA, Canada, Australia, Japa

Cover: Foto ©Andreas Hilbeck / pixelio.de

Manufactured and distributed by brebook publishing software
(www.brebook.com)

Thomas Annan

# The painted windows of Glasgow Cathedral

# Photographs

of the

## Painted Windows

in

## Glasgow Cathedral

by

## Thomas Annan.

THE

# PAINTED WINDOWS

OF

## GLASGOW CATHEDRAL.

SERIES OF FORTY-THREE PHOTOGRAPHS,

TAKEN BY

### THOMAS ANNAN

GLASGOW:
PUBLISHED BY THOMAS ANNAN,
*Photographer, 202 Hope Street.*
1867.

HER MOST GRACIOUS MAJESTY

The Queen,

AND

THE NOBLEMEN AND GENTLEMEN, DONORS OF THE PAINTED WINDOWS

IN

GLASGOW CATHEDRAL,

THIS WORK

IS MOST RESPECTFULLY DEDICATED,

BY

THOMAS ANNAN.

# PREFATORY NOTICE.

＊

The people of Glasgow are justly proud of their Cathedral; it was saved by them from destruction when other ecclesiastical edifices of the same description in Scotland were cast to the ground. Thus preserved, the Cathedral has of late years been carefully restored; and, with the exception perhaps of some of the modern oak fittings, the restorations have been carried out with judgment and good taste. On the completion of the repairs, it was suggested by Mr. Matheson, architect to Her Majesty's Board of Works in Scotland, that the windows should be filled with painted glass. Negotiations were commenced with this object, and, after some preliminary steps had been taken, a Committee of noblemen and gentlemen was appointed, and it was resolved at a meeting of Subscribers that a harmonious plan of illustration, suggested by the secretary of the Committee, should be carried out. The Committee, after much inquiry and deliberation, resolved to intrust the whole of the windows to the Royal establishment for Glass-painting at Munich, and some of the leading artists of the Munich school agreed to supply designs.

This series of Photographs of the Painted Windows of the Nave and Choir, has been printed from negatives taken from the windows since their erection. In a few instances it has not been possible to place the camera in a position to obtain a favourable representation, but the majority of the prints have been successfully produced. Impressions of these Photographs were forwarded to the late distinguished President of the Royal Academy in London (Sir Charles L. Eastlake), who in acknowledging them remarked, " I find a most comprehensive series of subjects, well selected, and in general extremely well treated. The only point on which I can offer no opinion is the colour and the general impression on the eye. Independently of the merit of the designs—independently of the quality of the work—I confess that I am astonished at the quantity. That such extensive works should have been planned and carried to completion, supposes great energy and perseverance." Photography, as yet, can convey no true idea of colour, and of the general effect on the eye of the original works; but, on the other hand, it is successful in representing the design and composition, the drawing of the figures and of the draperies, for the excellence of which these now celebrated windows are in most instances so remarkable, and so far above all other works of the same description lately erected in Great Britain. The first of the series of painted windows, in the western front, was finished and placed in November, 1859; and, in October, 1864, the whole of those in the nave and choir were completed, containing one hundred and twenty-three Bible subjects, designed by ten artists of reputation—amongst whom are some of the most distinguished of the German school. The names of the artists are appended to the Photographs, and those of Heinrich von Hess, Mauritz von Schwinde, and Johann von Schraudolph, may be specially noticed. The first window in the nave—the subject of which is Adam—is designed by Franz Fries, a pupil of Von Kaulbach, and an artist of remarkable powers. The veteran Chevalier Maximilian Ainmiller, architectural painter, inspector of the Royal Glass-painting establishment at Munich, composed the ornamental portions, and directed the entire execution of the work in glass.

It is hoped that this series of Photographs will prove interesting, not only to the donors of the windows, but to many others who appreciate the beautiful art of glass-painting. The windows undoubtedly constitute the greatest work of the kind undertaken in Great Britain, excelling all others in the completeness of the plan, and the unity of purpose with which it has been carried out.

Glasgow, *April* 1865.

INTERIOR OF GLASGOW CATHEDRAL.

From the Lower Church

EAST WINDOW

THE FOUR EVANGELISTS

SOUTH TRANSEPT
THE TYPES AND ANTITYPES OF OUR LORD

No. 4. Nave.

ISAAC

Designed by ALEXANDER STRACHAN

The Gift of Mrs. Ferguson

No. 3. No. 1
JACOB

No. 5. Transept

AARON AND MIRIAM

HANNAH AND SAMUEL

Designed by FRANK JONES

The Gift of Constance Katharine Richardson of Dunsmore

Seite 49. No. 49.
SAUL.

No. 18. Nave

F L I S K A

Designed by E. Steinheil

The Gift of James Morris, Esq. of Belladrum, and of
Alexander Cunninghame, Esq. of Craigends

No. 19. Nave
DANIEL.

No. 80. Nave.

EDUCATION.

Designed by HENRY AIKMAN(?)

The Gift of FREDERICK CRAWFORD, Esq.

No. 1, China.

PARABLE OF THE SOWER

No. 4. Sheet

ASK AND IT SHALL BE GIVEN YOU.

Designed by E. Sieberts.

No. 1.
THE GOOD AND FAITHFUL SERVANT

No. V. Essex.

"SUFFER LITTLE CHILDREN TO COME UNTO ME."

No. 10, Choir

THE RESURRECTION

No. 8, EAST WINDOW.

JAMES AND PHILIP

Designed by Henry Atkinson.
The Gift of the Misses Robertson Thomson.

No. 8, LIGHT WINDOW

BARTHOLOMEW AND THOMAS

Designed by HENRY HOLIDAY

The Gift of the EARL OF BEAUCHAMP

No. 5. LADY CHAPEL.
SIMON AND MATTHIAS

No. 6. LADY CHAPEL.

PAUL AND BARNABAS.

www.ingramcontent.com/pod-product-compliance
Lightning Source LLC
Chambersburg PA
CBHW020302090426
42735CB00009B/1191